Cheese-Roll RACES

Rob Waring, *Series Editor*

HEINLE
CENGAGE Learning™

Australia • Brazil • Japan • Korea • Mexico • Singapore • Spain • United Kingdom • United States

Words to Know

This story is set in England, in the United Kingdom. It happens in the town of Brockworth [brɒkwɜrθ].

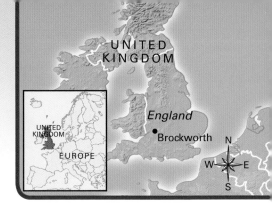

A **At the Races.** Here are some words you will see in the story. Complete the definitions with words in the box.

cheer	prize	route
crowd	race	spectators

1. The road or way you follow to get from one place to another place is a _____.

2. An event in which people try to be the fastest to do something is a _____.

3. To shout loudly to encourage someone is to _____.

4. A large group of people is a _____.

5. _____ are the people who are watching a sporting event, show, etc.

6. A _____ is something that is given to someone who wins a competition.

B Cheese-Rolling Races. Read the paragraph and look at the picture. Then match each word to the correct definition.

In England, many towns have traditional competitions. In them, competitors usually try to win a game or contest. However, the annual cheese-rolling race in Brockworth is a little unusual. At the start of the race, someone rolls a wheel of cheese down a very steep hill. Then, the competitors run after the cheese. The first person to reach the bottom of the hill is the winner.

1. competition _____	**a.** going up or down very suddenly
2. competitor _____	**b.** move quickly in a circular motion
3. annual _____	**c.** person who takes part in a race or contest
4. roll _____	**d.** one time every year
5. wheel of cheese _____	**e.** a large, round piece of cheese
6. steep _____	**f.** an organized event in which people try to be the best or fastest

The Annual Cheese-Rolling Race

C heese-rolling has been a tradition in the town of Brockworth since the early 1800s. But what happens in this old and locally famous competition? It's quite simple, really. First, the competitors come together at the top of a hill named 'Cooper's Hill.' The **slope**[1] of the hill is very steep—almost 45 degrees! And after that? They wait, but wait for what?

_____

[1]**slope:** the amount of difference between a high area and a lower area

🎧 CD 2, Track 09

FINISH

Cooper's Hill has a very steep slope!

What's the Main Idea?

1. What is the main idea of the paragraph on page 7?

2. How does the cheese-rolling competition work?

They wait for someone to push a very large wheel of cheese down the hill. The competitors then run very quickly after it. The cheese may reach up to **40 miles**[2] per hour. The competitors go pretty fast, too! The first one to the bottom of the hill wins. What's the prize for such an unusual event? It's the wheel of cheese—of course!

---

[2]**40 miles:** 64.3 kilometers

The first winner of the day in this year's competition is Craig Brown, a **pub**[3] worker. He's happy to be the winner, but he's also very tired. What did he do to win the race? Craig says that his plan was simple; the most important thing is just to continue running. "Keep [on] going," he says, "and try to get your **balance**[4] back." He then adds, "It's steeper than you could ever think. You'd have to run down there to really believe how steep it is!"

---

[3]**pub:** place where drinks and food are served
[4]**balance:** ability to stand up and not fall over due to unequal weight

Many people enjoy the cheese-rolling races of Brockworth. However, the race can be dangerous. You never know the route the cheese will take as it rolls down the hill. A few years ago, 30 people were **injured**[5] in an **accident**[6] at a race. One of the cheeses rolled down the hill too quickly and suddenly went into the crowd. Some of the spectators were hit by the cheese. Now, the competition route has **crash barriers.**[7] They protect the crowd from the cheese—and from the competitors!

---

[5]**injure:** cause bodily harm to a person or animal
[6]**accident:** a bad thing which happens without warning
[7]**crash barrier:** short wall along a competition route to protect spectators

Crash barriers protect the spectators at the races.

It's not just the spectators who get injured, the competitors do as well. This is especially true when the weather is very cold. There are also more injuries when there hasn't been much rain before the race. One organizer for the event explains, "It's when the ground is really hard…that's when the injuries are going to happen."

But the hard ground doesn't seem to stop the competitors. Every year there are a lot of people who follow Craig Brown's suggestion; they just 'keep on going' down Cooper's Hill. But what about Craig? How did he do in the remaining cheese-rolling races?

Well, Craig's plan to just 'keep on going' unfortunately failed. When he tried to keep on going in the second race, he lost his balance and fell—again and again! At the time, he was trying to get the competition's version of a 'double play'. He wanted to win two cheese wheels in one day. But instead of going home with a 'double cheese,' Craig went home with only one cheese, and maybe a few **bruises**![8]

---

[8]**bruises:** dark purple or black marks on the skin from an injury

So, what drives these runners? What makes them do it? Are they **crazy**?[9] One cheese runner thinks they may be. "It is dangerous," he says as he looks at the very steep slope of Cooper's Hill. "If I'm running down [the hill], [I] must be crazy. Yeah, I must be crazy…" he decides with a smile.

_____

[9]**crazy:** not having a good mind; not sensible

The cheese racers of Brockworth may just be crazy. However, the crowds keep on cheering, and the competitors keep on running—year after year. It seems that a lot of people are very happy to try this dangerous run. Is it for the **fame**?[10] Is it for the fun? We may never know, but you can almost be sure of one thing; it's not only for the prize. It's more than just cheese that makes people want to win Brockworth's annual cheese-rolling race!

---

[10]**fame:** being known for one's achievements or skills

What do you think?

1. Do you think the cheese runners are crazy?

2. Would you like to be a competitor in this cheese-rolling competition? Why or why not?

3. Do you participate in any activities which other people might think are 'crazy'?

After You Read

1. On page 4, what does 'locally' mean?
   A. traditional
   B. in the area
   C. ancient
   D. totally

2. How long has the competition been happening?
   A. forty-five years
   B. less than two hundred years
   C. over two hundred years
   D. 1800 years

3. What is the goal of the competition?
   A. to be the first person down the hill
   B. to follow the competitors
   C. to be quicker than the cheese
   D. to roll cheese down a hill

4. On page 7, 'one' refers to a:
   A. wheel of cheese
   B. prize
   C. winner
   D. person

5. Choose the best heading for page 8.
   A. Tired But Happy Loser
   B. Hill Is Not So Bad
   C. Pub Worker Gets Cheese
   D. Balance Is Unimportant

6. How does Craig Brown describe the competition?
   A. simple, but steep
   B. unbelievably tiring
   C. harder than it looks
   D. easy if you don't stop

7. On page 10, 'it' is referring to the:
    A. race
    B. route
    C. cheese
    D. danger

8. One time the cheese crashed _____ a crowd of spectators.
    A. on
    B. in
    C. with
    D. into

9. When are injuries likely to occur during the races?
    A. if the weather is warm
    B. if the ground is too hard
    C. if it has rained before the race
    D. all of the above

10. What happens to Craig Brown in the second race?
    A. He loses his balance.
    B. He gets a double play.
    C. He wins the cheese.
    D. He is badly injured.

11. What's the purpose of page 16?
    A. to prove that the competition is safe
    B. to show the competitors are unhappy
    C. to prove that the town is crazy
    D. none of the above

12. What does the writer probably think about the competition?
    A. The spectators cheer too much.
    B. The race is too dangerous.
    C. The competitors like the fame and fun.
    D. The prize is very good cheese.

BED RACING
It Isn't Crazy After All

Bed racing is becoming more popular in certain areas of the U.S. A bed race is a competition where teams of people push beds along a specific route. The route often goes through the middle of a city or town. The competing teams attempt to roll their beds along the route faster than anyone else. However, these are not just any beds! Racing beds often have very big wheels and the competitors sometimes paint them in some very interesting ways.

Most bed races are about having fun and raising money for the community.

2007 Race Results

	1st Place	2nd Place	3rd Place	Last Place
Team	*Sleepwalkers*	*Morning Suns*	*Fast Times*	*Sleeping Beauties*
Time	4 minutes, 31 seconds	4 minutes, 42 seconds	5 minutes, 10 seconds	14 minutes, 14 seconds

The teams build their own beds and practice for weeks before the race. However, race organizers often have firm rules about building and racing beds. For example: the beds must be a certain size, they can't have an engine, and they must have four wheels. In addition, there must be no more than six people pushing the bed and only one person can sit in the bed.

As long as the teams follow the rules, they can use their imaginations for everything else. Some beds are covered with flowers. Others beds look like crazy boats. To add to the fun, people often wear strange and unusual clothing.

On race days, large crowds of spectators come to cheer for their favorite team. These members of the community usually give money to their favorite team. However, the money doesn't go to the team members. It goes to organizations that help people in need. In the past, bed races have raised lots of money to provide health care for children and to help homeless people. At the end of the race, teams are often listed in a chart like the one above. Most of these teams don't even get a prize for winning. These bed races are obviously not serious events. The important thing is to raise money for the community and to have fun.

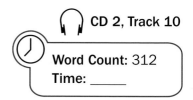

CD 2, Track 10

Word Count: 312
Time: _____

Vocabulary List

accident (10)
annual (3, 18)
balance (8, 15)
bruise (15)
cheer (2, 18)
competition (3, 4, 6, 7, 10, 15, 19)
competitor (3, 4, 7, 10, 12, 18, 19)
crash barrier (10)
crazy (16, 18, 19)
crowd (2, 10, 18)
fame (18)
injure (10, 12)
prize (2, 7, 18)
pub (8)
race (2, 3, 8, 10)
roll (3, 4, 6, 10, 12, 18, 19)
route (2, 10)
slope (4, 5, 16)
spectator (2, 10, 12)
steep (3, 4, 8, 16)
wheel of cheese (3, 7, 15)